BASIC CHROMATIC HARMONICA

BY PHIL DUNCAN

Online Audio   www.melbay.com/30563MEB

MEL BAY

QWIKGUIDE®

Contents

Title	Audio Track	Page
Introduction		4
Some Folks Do	1	5
New World Theme	2	6
Ode To Joy	3	6
For He's A Jolly Good Fellow	4	7
Mozart Air	5	7
Danube Waves	6	8
The Coventry Carol	7	8
Nobody Knows The Trouble I've Seen	8	9
Old Joe Clark	9	9
Grandfather's Clock	10	10
Scales (Diatonic, Chromatic, Blues)	11	10
Walking Boogie In C	12	11
Look Down That Lonesome Road	13	11
America, The Beautiful	14	12
Sarabande	15	12
Dark Eyes	16	13
An Evening Prayer	17	13
Beautiful Dreamer	18	14
By The Light Of The Silvery Moon	19	15
Cantabile By Sain-Saens	20	16
Ciribiribin	21	17
Deep River	22	18
Drigo's Serenade	23	18
Edvard Grieg's Piano Concerto Theme	24	19
Expectation Waltz	25	20
Fantasie - Impromptu	26	21
Give My Regards To Broadway	27	22
Graceful Waltz	28	23
House Of The Rising Sun	29	24

Contents

Title	Audio Track	Page
Joshua Fit The Battle Of Jericho	30	25
Let Me Call You Sweetheart	31	26
Melody In F	32	27
My Old Kentucky Home	33	28
Nocturne Op. 9, No. 2	34	29
Opening Love Theme, Romeo And Juliet	35	29
Over the Waves	36	30
Prayer Of Thanksgiving	37	31
Sometimes I Feel Like A Motherless Child	38	32
Symphony No. 7 (2nd Movement)	39	33
Waltz By Mozart	40	34
Waltz Op. 34, No. 2 (Chopin)	41	34
While Strolling Thru The Park One Day	42	35
Whispering Hope	43	36

Introduction

This Basic Chromatic Harmonica book gives you easy access to playing harmonica. This book will use the 12 or 16 hole chromatic harmonica in the key of C. This book is written in standard musical notation as well as tablature. Tablature is expressed in arrows and numbers. When the arrow points up, you blow, when the arrow points down, you draw/inhale. The number indicates which hole to blow in or draw out. The circled numbers tell you to push in the slide button on the right for sharps or flats. The chromatic harmonica can play in any key. Chromatic means it can play all 12 tones of the scale.

Chromatic Harmonica Note Chart

UPPER-CASE LETTERS are blow;

lower case letters are draw.

with the slide out there are three complete octaves of "C" scale.

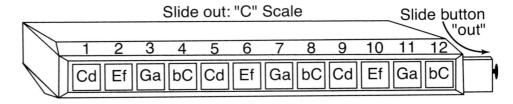

With the slide in, all the tones are sharp, except hole 12 draw. These tones are raised a half step, making three complete octaves of "C♯" scale.

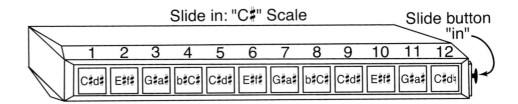

Holding the Harmonica

Hold the harmonica firmly in the left hand with hole number one to the left. The left-hand fingers should lie along the upper part of the harmonica and the thumb along the lower part. The right hand should be cupped around the back of the harmonica with the right-hand index finger positioned on the slide button. The heel of both hands should remain together.

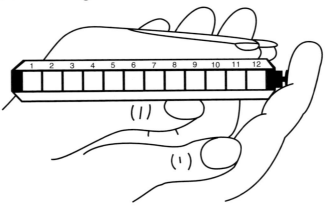

Vibrato

If you open and close the right hand, a wavering tone will begin. Some performers use the last three fingers of the left hand, moving them up and down, to create a vibrato. Puffing air as you play, both blow and draw, in a steady manner while playing a sustained tone will create a vibrato.

Tongue and Lip Blocking

Tongue blocking is normally used to play chromatic harmonica. This is a technique in which the tongue usually covers the two left adjacent holes so the air coming down the right inside of the mouth will enter only one hole to the right of the tongue.

There are two ways of blocking out undesired tones on the harmonica. Beginners usually use the "lip blocking," simply pursing the lips so that only one tone sounds.

Lip Blocking

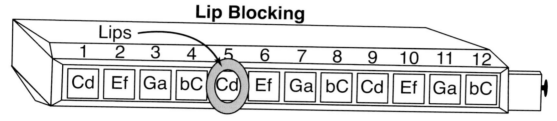

The second way is to "tongue block." The tongue blocks the unwanted holes on the left, while allowing the air stream to move down the inside right of the mouth into a single hole.

Tongue Blocking

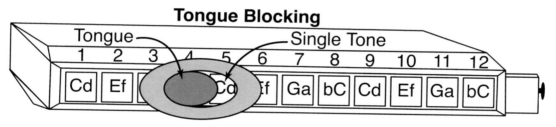

SOME FOLKS DO

5

NEW WORLD THEME

A. Dvorak

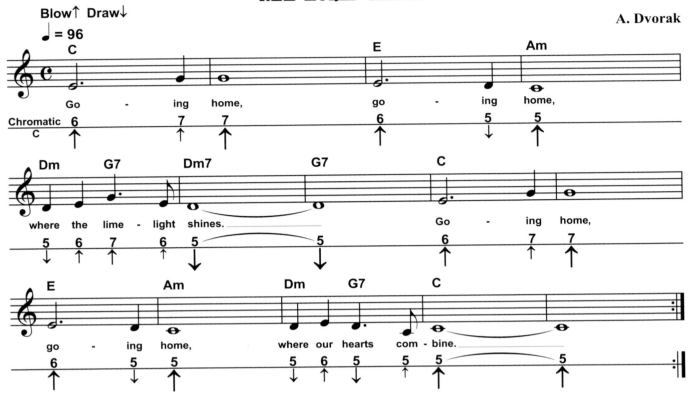

ODE TO JOY

Beethoven

FOR HE'S A JOLLY GOOD FELLOW

Traditional

MOZART AIR

W. A. Mozart

DANUBE WAVES

Ivanovici

THE COVENTRY CAROL

English Melody

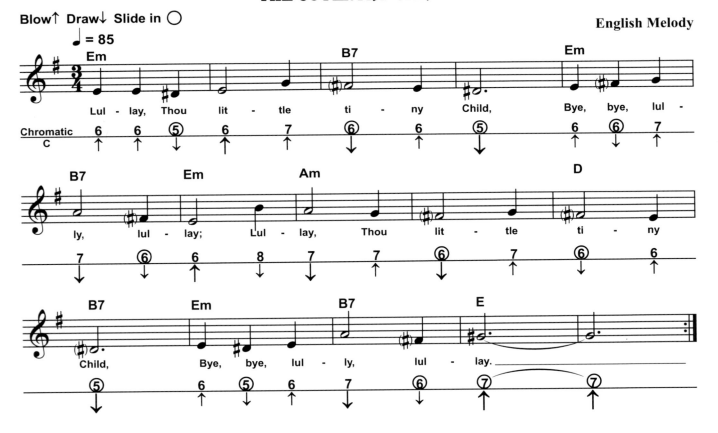

NOBODY KNOWS THE TROBLE I'VE SEEN

OLD JOE CLARK

9

GRANDFATHER'S CLOCK

Folk Tune

C DIATONIC SCALE

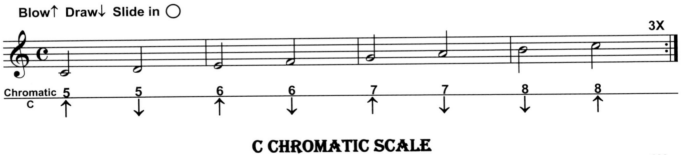

C CHROMATIC SCALE

C BLUES SCALE

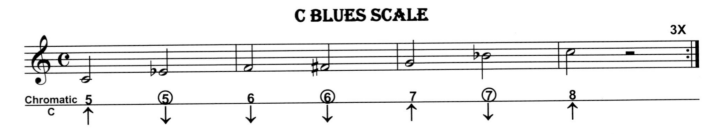

WALKING BOOGIE IN C

Blow↑ Draw↓ Slide in ◯

Phil Duncan

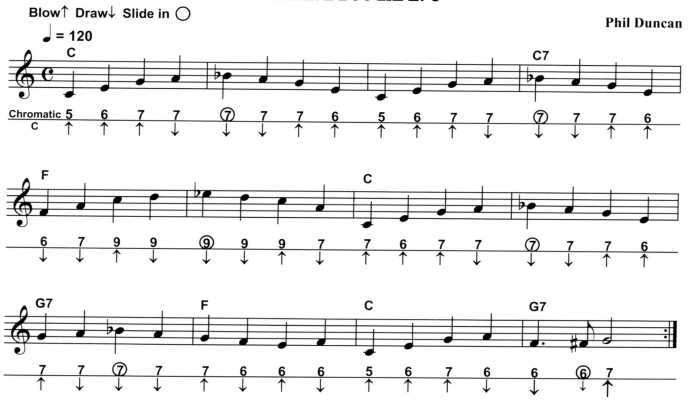

LOOK DOWN THAT LONESOME ROAD

Blow↑ Draw↓ Slide in ◯

Arr. Phil Duncan
Traditional

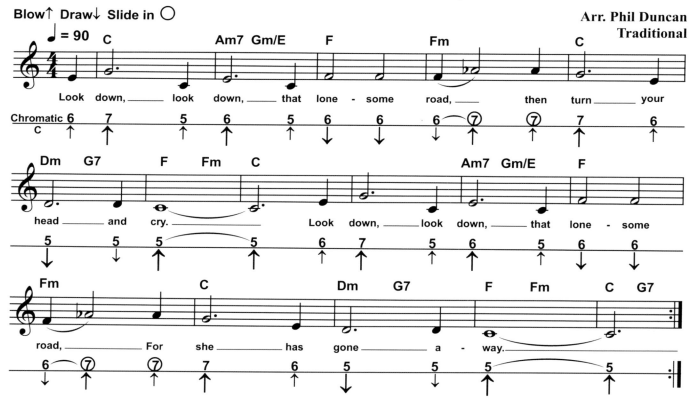

11

AMERICA, THE BEAUTIFUL

S. A. Ward

Blow↑ Draw↓ Slide in ◯

SARABANDE

G. F. Handel

Blow↑ Draw↓ Slide in ◯

DARK EYES

AN EVENING PRAYER

BEAUTIFUL DREAMER

Arr. Phil Duncan

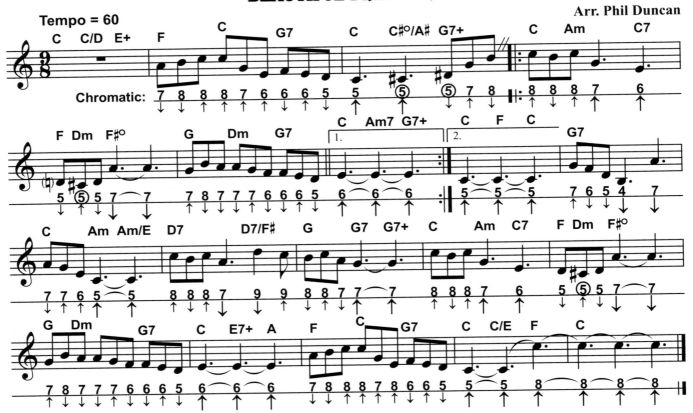

BY THE LIGHT OF THE SILVERY MOON

Arr. Phil Duncan

15

CANTABILE BY SAIN-SAENS

Arr. Phil Duncan

CIRIBIRIBIN

A. Pestalozza
Arr. Phil Duncan

17

DEEP RIVER

Arr. Phil Duncan

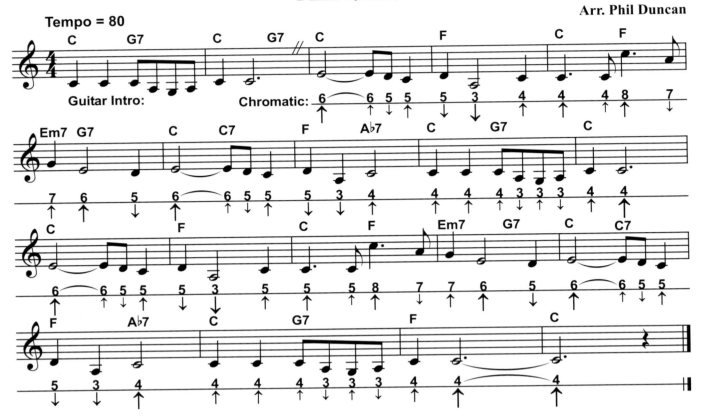

DRIGO'S SERENADE

R. Drigo
Arr. Phil Duncan

EDVARD GRIEG'S PIANO CONCERTO THEME

Edvard Grieg
Arr. Phil Duncan

Tempo = 120
Intro:

19

EXPECTATION WALTZ

Arr. Phil Duncan

FANTASIE-IMPROMPTU

F. Chopin
Arr. Phil Duncan

Tempo = 90

Guitar Intro:

Chromatic:

21

GIVE MY REGARDS TO BROADWAY

George M. Cohan
Arr. Phil Duncan

GRACEFUL WALTZ

Johannes Brahms
Arr. Phil Duncan

Tempo = 100

HOUSE OF THE RISING SUN

Tempo = 110

Arr. Phil Duncan

JOSHUA FIT THE BATTLE OF JERICHO

Tempo = 120

Intro:

Arr. Phil Duncan

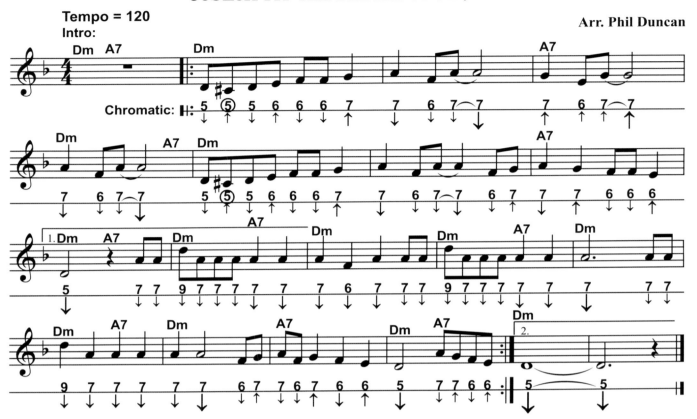

LET ME CALL YOU SWEETHEART

Whitson
Arr. Phil Duncan

Tempo = 100

MELODY IN F

Anton Rubinstein
Arr. Phil Duncan

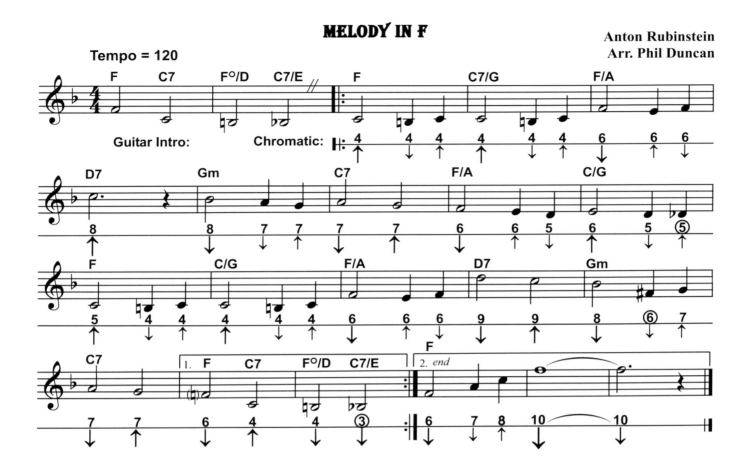

MY OLD KENTUCKY HOME

Tempo = 120

Arr. Phil Duncan

28

NOCTURNE OP. 9, NO. 2

F. Chopin
Arr. Phil Duncan

OPENING LOVE THEME, ROMEO AND JULIET

Peter Tchaikovsky
Arr. Phil Duncan

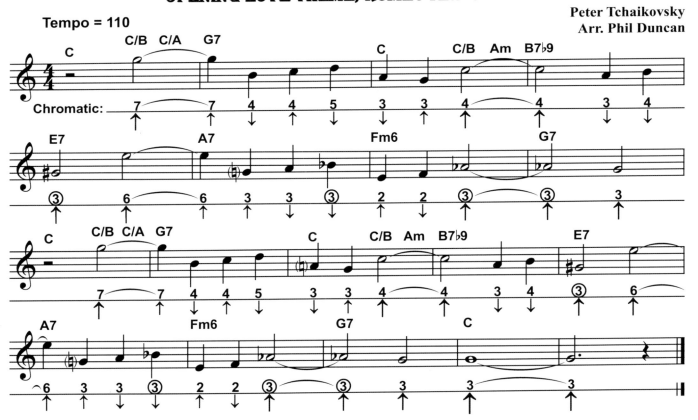

OVER THE WAVES

30

PRAYER OF THANKSGIVING

Dutch
Arr. Phil Duncan

31

SOMETIMES I FEEL LIKE A MOTHERLESS CHILD

Tempo = 64

Arr. Phil Duncan

SYMPHONY NO. 7 (2ND MOVEMENT)

Ludwig Van Beethoven
Arr. Phil Duncan

Tempo = 100

33

WALTZ BY MOZART

W. A. Mozart
Arr. Phil Duncan

Tempo = 120

Chromatic:

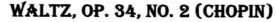

WALTZ, OP. 34, NO. 2 (CHOPIN)

F. Chopin
Arr. Phil Duncan

Tempo = 90

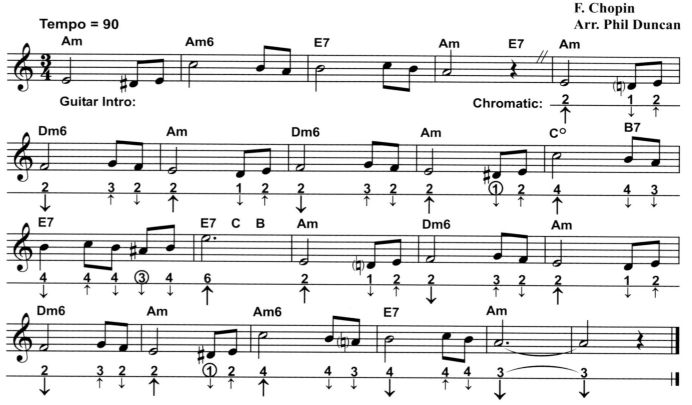

WHILE STROLLING THRU THE PARK ONE DAY

Arr. Phil Duncan

Tempo = 105

Piano Intro:

Chromatic:

day. In the mer-ry, mer-ry month of May. I was

tak-en by sur-prise, by a pair of ro-guish eyes. In a mo-ment, my poor heart was stole a-

way. We ling-er'd there be-neath the trees. Her

voice was like the fra-grant breeze. We talked of hap-py love un-

till the stars a-bove When her lov-ing "yes" she gave my heart to please.

WHISPERING HOPE

Arr. Phil Duncan